From Settlement to Society

VOLUME 3

From Settlement to Society

Archaeological Treasures of the Ocmulgee Corridor

DANIEL PHILIP BIGMAN
EDITED BY S. HEATHER DUNCAN

MERCER UNIVERSITY OCMULGEE SERIES
VOLUME 3

MERCER UNIVERSITY PRESS
MACON, GEORGIA

MUP/ P655

© 2022 by Mercer University Press
Published by Mercer University Press
1501 Mercer University Drive
Macon, Georgia 31207
All rights reserved

26 25 24 23 22   5 4 3 2 1

Books published by Mercer University Press are printed on
acid-free paper that meets the requirements of the American
National Standard for Information Sciences—Permanence of
Paper for Printed Library Materials.

Printed and bound in the United States.

Text is set in Meta Pro Serif, 10.5/13;
display is set in Clarendon Text pro;
captions are set in Meta Pro, 8/9

Book design by Burt&Burt.

ISBN 978-0-88146-865-6

Cataloging-in-Publication Data is available
from the Library of Congress

Table of Contents

Photo by Sharman Ayoub.

Acknowledgments

To Cathie Bigman, my loving and patient wife, whose constant support sustained me through the research process.

Many thanks to Sharman Ayoub, whose photos have enriched this book tremendously.

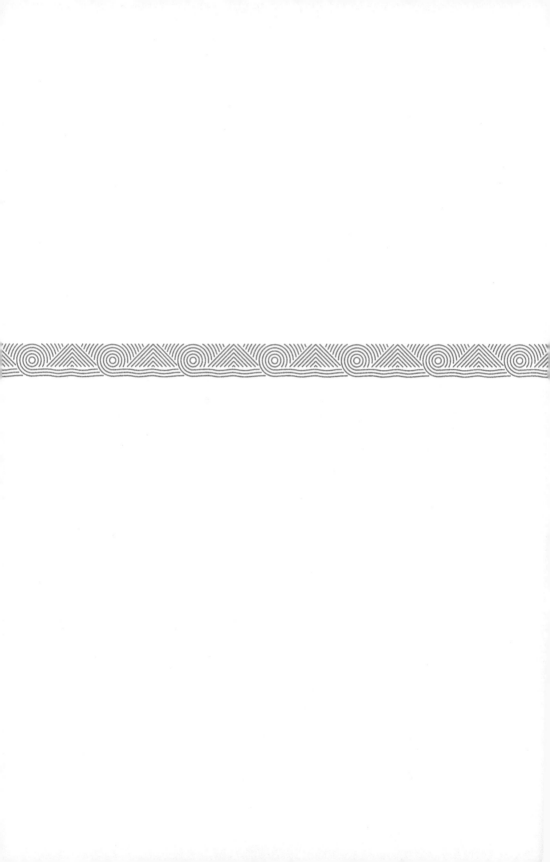

From Settlement to Society

VOLUME 3

Macon is visible from the top of the Great Temple Mound as a storm approaches at sunset.
Photo by Sharman Ayoub.

CHAPTER 1

Where We Live Shapes How We Live

Mapping the Evolution of Ocmulgee

From the Great Temple Mound at Ocmulgee Mounds National Historical Park, the Macon skyline recedes into the sunset, and cars buzz dimly from the interstate. The impact of modern civilization is apparent even from the solitude of these seven hundred acres of rippling grass and reflected sky. Yet the overlap is perhaps fitting: the Ocmulgee mounds themselves represent one of the first, most monumental marks early man made upon the Southeastern landscape.

The cluster of huge mounds was built more than a thousand years ago by the Mississippian culture, the ancestors of the modern Muscogee (Creek) tribe. The mounds remained a cultural crossroads to the time of earliest European contact. Spanish explorer Hernando de Soto passed nearby, and early-American naturalist William Bartram described them.

The mounds and related cultural sites were the subject of one of America's largest-scale archaeology projects conducted during the Great Depression. Under the Works Progress Administration and other federal jobs programs, eight thousand men and women dug trenches and helped map the footprint of surrounding settlements, directed by archaeologist Arthur R. Kelly. Yet many gaps remained in our understanding of this Mississippian-era settlement.

This University of Georgia research conducted by Daniel Philip Bigman, first published in 2012, focused on the where people lived over the centuries in which the mounds were built. The study expands on these findings to explore *why*: what do settlement patterns tell us about the society and how the community evolved?

Bigman used a variety of field survey and data-analysis methods to gather evidence. He applied the quickest and simplest techniques—such as global positioning markers and tests of underground conductivity—over large areas. He reserved more time-consuming approaches—such as ground-penetrating radar and sifting soil—in smaller areas to gather more specific information.

In addition, the study categorized the types of ceramic artifacts found at the site over time. It analyzed how often these were found and in which soil layers. These efforts produced a new approach that divides Ocmulgee settlement history into five stages. Each stage reflects changes in the size of the community, relationships between households, and construction of public architecture.

Finally, the research places Ocmulgee's development in the context of other large Early Mississippian mound centers and communities in the geographic region.

Most broadly, Bigman argues that Ocmulgee is not a "mystery"—something odd and different—but rather a case study that can be used for several purposes. First, it is helpful in understanding the interactions among Mississippian communities. Second,

A sunset sky over the Great Temple Mound. *Photo by Sharman Ayoub.*

Ocmulgee demonstrates how the struggle for power shaped an individual settlement while leadership roles evolved and social inequality fluctuated.

Ecological Setting

Ocmulgee Mounds National Historical Park is located in the city limits of Macon, Georgia, next to the Ocmulgee River. The river, whose source is near Atlanta, meanders south past the mounds and eventually turns east toward the Atlantic Ocean. It joins the Oconee and Ohoopee Rivers to form the Altamaha River system, Georgia's largest watershed.

The Ocmulgee Mounds are located at the fall line, the shore of an ancient sea. Archaeology is affected by the resulting geology of the region, so archaeologists look for traces of human settlement both at the surface and below ground. Artifacts are often buried in layers of soil that were deposited over time by flooding, erosion, or volcanic activity. An artifact's location within the soil provides clues about its age and sometimes about how it was used.

Ocmulgee is located in what seems to have been a preferred zone for Mississippian mound centers. In the South Atlantic region, these were often situated on a river along the fall line, which offered natural resources of both the piedmont and coastal

An Aerial view of Ocmulgee Mounds National Historical Park. *Photo by Sharman Ayoub.*

The rich Ocmulgee floodplain stretches almost to the base of the mounds.
Photo by Sharman Ayoub.

plain. These rivers were surrounded by rich floodplain soils, good for farming. River shoals provided rich fisheries.

Bibb County has a temperate but moist climate, probably very similar to the period when the mounds were built. Common ecosystems of the current Ocmulgee Mounds National Historical Park include a variety of hardwood forests, mixed pinewoods, meadows, and mowed grass areas.

Early History of Human Settlement

Humans have occupied the Ocmulgee Plateau for seventeen thousand years. Clovis points—hunting tools resembling a large spearhead—have been found that show humans hunted the area during the Paleo-Indian period, which lasted from roughly 13,500 to 8000 B.C.

Ceramic remains show Native Americans reoccupying Ocmulgee several times during the Late Archaic and Woodland periods. The earliest farming, ceramics, and regional trade began during the Archaic period (8000 to 1000 B.C.). The following Woodland period (until 1000 A.D.) saw the development of more socially and politically complex settlements around farms. These communities were involved in more extensive trade networks.

The Great Temple Mound sits among a field of wildflowers in early summer.
Photo by Sharman Ayoub.

The largest settlement at Ocmulgee appeared during the Early Mississippian period (from around 1000 A.D. to 1200 A.D.). Every mound at the site appears to date to this time. Ocmulgee might be the largest mound site in Georgia and is one of the largest in the eastern United States.

A historic Creek Indian town developed at Ocmulgee after this tribe began migrating to the area to take advantage of trading opportunities. The Creek town surrounded a British trading house established by merchants from the Carolinas, which was rediscovered during excavations in the 1930s. The Creek abandoned this town sometime soon after the Yamasee War of 1715.

Layout of Ocmulgee Settlement

There are about eight mounds at the Ocmulgee town site, which is also called the Macon Plateau. The largest mound, commonly called the Great Temple Mound, is located at the southern tip of the main bluff closest to the river. It's about sixteen yards tall and one hundred yards square at the base. Significant space separates it from the smaller mounds, except for the Lesser Temple Mound about ninety-eight yards to the north. Three other mounds—Funeral, Dunlap, and McDougal Mounds—are located on adjacent bluffs to the west and north along with a few smaller

5

This image shows the locations of major mounds at Ocmulgee. They are designated by letters here, but some are better known by common names. These are: Mound A: Great Temple Mound; Mound B: Lesser Temple Mound; Mound C: Funeral Mound; and Mound D: Cornfield Mound. *Graphic by Daniel Bigman.*

mounds. However, mounds outside the boundaries of the modern historical park might also have been associated with Ocmulgee.

Near the Cornfield Mound is the well-known reconstructed Earth Lodge, a ceremonial chamber with the original clay floor featuring the silhouette of an eagle. After it stopped being used as a council chamber, the lodge might have been converted into a building platform.

An 1806 survey by the US government identified three mounds on the Fort Hawkins bluff outside the modern-day park. They would have been about 440 yards from the nearest mound in the park. Fort Hawkins, perched at the edge of Indian territory, served as an important US trading post with the Creek Indians. The Fort Hawkins mounds have never been adequately dated, but Early Mississippian ceramics have been recovered there. Including these mounds raises the total possible number of Ocmulgee mounds to twelve. Bigman divided the surviving mounds and surrounding land into six general areas for this study.

Paving the Way: Kelly's Work

Most of what is known about the layout of Ocmulgee we owe to investigations directed by archaeologist Arthur Kelly during the Great Depression. More excavations occurred at Ocmulgee than at any other archaeological site in Georgia; in fact, it was one of the most extensive archaeological projects ever undertaken in the United States.

Kelly's work, sponsored by the Civil Works Administration starting in December 1933, continued after funding shifted a few months later to the Federal Emergency Relief Administration. In the middle of January 1934, the project employed 274 workers. By July 1935, that number had increased to about seven hundred in the Macon area.

Despite frequent visits from notable archaeologists such as William S. Webb and Thomas M. N. Lewis, Kelly still did not have professionally trained assistants. James A. Ford, a twenty-two-year-old undergraduate student at the time, was Kelly's only assistant until June 1936, when six additional graduate assistants arrived in Macon. Kelly continued to direct excavations at Ocmulgee until August 1938, when he left to work at Chaco Canyon in New Mexico. The Ocmulgee site is so large and rich that much

Left, archaeologist Arthur Kelly, with pipe, supervised the Depression-era excavations at the Ocmulgee Mounds. Right, "Mr. Jackson" sketches the finds in 1938 during the Ocmulgee excavation project. *Photos courtesy of National Park Service.*

remains unexcavated, as are many culturally related sites along the Ocmulgee River.

The scope of the federal relief project and the lack of trained support staff during so much of the work meant the results weren't well recorded. Almost ninety years later, many of Kelly's finds haven't been reported and many of the artifacts still haven't been analyzed.

Gordon Willey excavated the Southeast Plateau section of Ocmulgee in 1937 and 1938 as part of his stratified survey. This is the best-documented and most systematic work performed at Ocmulgee during the New Deal era. Unfortunately, it remains one of the least reported.

Kelly published his only report regarding Ocmulgee in 1938. He hoped to return to Macon and prepare additional reports on his findings, but he remained at Chaco Canyon for six years.

Charles Fairbanks published a paper on the earth lodges in 1945. About twenty years after Kelly's investigations, Fairbanks

WPA workers excavate near the Great Temple Mound at Ocmulgee.
Photo courtesy of National Park Service.

also wrote about artifacts analyzed from a single mound. It wasn't until the 1960s that the National Park Service arranged reports on the Depression-era excavations.

Despite the scale of these investigations, little was known about the layout of the Ocmulgee settlement when the UGA study was undertaken. The limited information on homes or domestic structures was the most significant barrier to mapping Ocmulgee and understanding the relationships among its social groups.

Kelly identified few houses. Archaeologists still don't have a clear understanding of how homes were spaced, how big they were, and how they related to public architecture.

Because the federal relief workers dug so many trenches, one might conclude that Kelly found most of the houses. But there are three problems with this argument: First, the unsupervised laborers easily could have overlooked evidence of structures, including postholes or baked-clay floors. Second, trenches might have been spaced too far apart (sixty meters, in some cases), leaving large enough gaps to completely miss buildings. Finally, the choice to focus trenches in the central area might have left outlying residential space unexplored.

While the Depression-era archaeological investigations were significant in many respects, their lack of documentation and scattershot analysis afterward leaves many gaps in our knowledge of the Ocmulgee settlement. The UGA study aimed to combine new investigations with analysis of previously recovered artifacts in order to explore how the Ocmulgee community functioned during its roughly 200 of settlement during the Early Mississippian period.

Later Excavations and Research

In the 1960s and '70s, some archaeologists analyzed and reported portions of the information gathered by Kelly. The National Park Service also conducted some small excavations at Ocmulgee over the years. These were mostly triggered by infrastructure projects that could affect archaeological remains. (Examples are paving and installing sewer lines or solar panels.)

Some of these NPS investigations uncovered ceramic fragments that were used in the UGA analysis. For instance, in 2000, the Park Service began archaeological testing in the Middle Plateau to prepare for building a pedestrian bridge. Unlike the previous WPA excavations, those conducted by the Park Service screened all the dirt removed. As a result, smaller pottery pieces were collected than had been discovered in the 1930s. The depths of these artifacts were better recorded. They were located within five separate layers, providing more reliable information about their likely age.

Building on Previous Interpretations of Human Settlement

Previous efforts have been made to interpret early human settlement at Ocmulgee. Archaeologists David Hally and Mark Williams, using preexisting studies, conducted the only site-wide analysis of the area and developed the most comprehensive map of Ocmulgee. Still, they acknowledged that it didn't show all the areas excavated and might not be completely accurate. This was mostly because of incomplete or missing field records.

Hally and Williams's goal was to summarize the architectural characteristics of Ocmulgee's buildings, speculate about their functions, and learn how they were laid out in relation to each other. They proposed that, unlike other major mound complexes of the area, Ocmulgee might have been built as a series of "sub-communities," each clustered around a mound and its plaza.

At many other Mississippian sites, such as Moundville and Toltec, the mounds were closer together. This led researchers to conclude that their mounds functioned as a single central anchor for the entire community, with homes surrounding a main plaza or group of neighboring plazas.

Cohokia Mounds in Illinois. *Photo courtesy Getty Images.*

But if the Ocmulgee Mounds, like those at Cahokia, anchored subcommunities, that might also indicate how those related to local government.

Archaeologist Jon Muller has suggested that council chambers such as those found at Ocmulgee were political meeting places where high-ranking citizens could wield influence, while chiefs functioned as figureheads with limited power. At these meeting places, members of different subgroups would come together to make decisions.

In contrast, other historians have argued that council chambers were spaces where powerful chiefs sought advice and culled favor, support, and loyalty from their most influential constituents.

The reality might be that the form of rule fluctuated over time between powerful and limited centralized leadership.

Moundville Archaeological Park in Alabama. *Photo courtesy University of Alabama.*

Archaeologists and ethnologists have made convincing arguments that societies of this era shifted socially and structurally.

Hally and Williams recognized that the Ocmulgee settlement lasted long enough to reflect changes in pottery making and town layout. They gaged when the mound areas were constructed, concluding that the Great Temple Mound and Lesser Temple Mound were built first. Then the Cornfield Mound and its lodge were built, along with some residential areas. All were enclosed by defensive ditches. Later, some of these were filled in, and the earliest mounds stopped being used for elite residences and temples. The other mounds were constructed later. Ocmulgee could be a good comparative case study for the development of Mississippian settlements, communities, and political structure.

Several recent studies of large archaeological sites from the Woodland and Mississippian periods have altered our understanding of how towns and their social structures evolve. From different perspectives, they all addressed the shifting relationship between population, town form, and the use of space. The UGA study was framed similarly.

Study questions

Within this context, the UGA study aimed to answer basic questions about Ocmulgee society: Where did people live, and when? Did Ocmulgee consist of subcommunities? Did the settlement layout change over time?

Almost all Mississippian communities featured multiple settlements integrated across a region. They also had some kind of institutionalized leadership. But these communities varied in origin, structure, layout, size, and other features. Leaders might have wielded varying amounts of centralized control over time.

Past researchers have suggested that the site plans of small settlements reflect family relationships, wealth, status, government, religion, and the division of labor among men and women. Put simply, patterns of where homes are built reveal important clues about how people relate to each other and the natural environment.

Bigman used archaeology to better understand power relationships at Ocmulgee. In particular, he wanted to know how subcommunities functioned in the larger social system. This study

A park ranger shares the history of the Ocmulgee Earth Lodge with visitors to Ocmulgee National Monument, now a national historical park. *Photo by Sharman Ayoub.*

sought to identify changing relationships between residential groups over the years.

The UGA study hypothesized that during some periods, the Ocmulgee settlement was governed through a traditional chiefdom model, with centralized decision-making. Other times in the settlement history were more socially and politically democratic.

Under the more centralized model, leaders had considerable power and influence over their towns. Social rank was important. Inequality was normal. Towns organized this way could build huge monuments requiring complex community planning.

Researchers detect variations in social rank through differences in the layout of homes and the artifacts found in them. Bigger homes, containing precious or exotic items, would be located closer to landmarks such as mounds and council chambers. Commoners would live farther away from this kind of public architecture.

Interior of the Ocmulgee Earth Lodge. *Photo by Sharman Ayoub.*

Conversely, during times of greater social equality and more democratic government, Bigman proposed that these physical markers would look different. Households would be around the same size, separated by open space to indicate group boundaries. They'd contain a similar amount of fine wares and unusual goods. And if power-sharing was common, each household would be about the same distance from public architecture. These archaeological patterns would reflect that although households and villages might have internal hierarchies, they worked together to achieve broad political, economic, or cultural goals.

Modern investigative tools would be needed to test these theories about a civilization deep in the past.

Deer graze a freshly mowed path at Ocmulgee Mounds National Historic Park. *Photo by Sharman Ayoub.*

CHAPTER 2

Tools of the Future Illuminate the Past

Survey Methods and Technology

The UGA study used a variety of sophisticated methods to unlock the underground secrets of the Mississippian settlement at Ocmulgee. These techniques were chosen to answer specific questions and to deal with the particular soils and landforms at the site.

The Ocmulgee Plateau presents many challenges to the modern archaeologist. Areas used by early humans are spread out. Some are widely separated from each other, and not all are part of the federal property of Ocmulgee Mounds National Historical Park. The ground surface and type of ground cover varies widely. Some areas have steep slopes, with considerable changes in elevation even over short distances.

Modern buildings, trails, and a railroad have been constructed on top of—and even through—mounds and underground features. Kelly's trenching in the 1930s left its own marks and might have obliterated some signs of early human habitation.

To cope with these challenges, the UGA study used many survey techniques. To further refine survey results, ceramics from previous excavations were analyzed.

Each survey method generally reveals information about a single physical property of the earth. Buried cultural features are often visible using one technique but not another. That's why using multiple methods usually provides greater insight. When pieced together, the results reveal a more precise picture of what is underground without having to dig it all up.

Huge archaeological excavations of early human settlements aren't feasible anymore. They are expensive and destructive to surface features. In addition, federal law now recognizes Native American ancestral rights and limits disturbance of Native American graves.

Luckily, modern technology allows archaeologists to map underground features and analyze spatial relationships without disturbing the ground much. These methods fall under the umbrella of "geophysical surveying."

The UGA study applied simple, fast techniques to survey large swaths of the landscape, reserving more time-consuming approaches for smaller areas where more detailed information was sought and for forested areas. Multiple techniques were used in several sections of the landscape to provide a clearer picture of underground features.

This chapter explains each geophysical survey technique in more detail.

GPS Topographic Survey

The UGA study used global positioning technology to collect information about the shape of the land surface. This created a grid of map points, allowing data to be specifically linked to the place where it was collected.

Surveying Ocmulgee Mounds National Historic Park with GPS. *Photo courtesy Daniel Bigman.*

To collect this information, Bigman used a GPS antenna attached to a pole on a specialized backpack. As the researcher walked, the antenna continuously collected data points every two seconds.

The goal of the topographic survey was to map the landscape and prominent archaeological features, such as mounds and ditches. This is a broad-brush approach; it doesn't find small variations that might indicate buried structures.

The study ended up including a total of 17,857 usable GPS points.

Magnetometer

A magnetometer records the earth's magnetic field strength. Archaeologists are interested in identifying variations in the earth's magnetic field strength which can be caused by changes in the subsurface, possibly from buried objects or features.

A magnetometer doesn't just identify metal objects. Prehistoric cultural features, such as hearths, pits, and postholes from buildings, produce magnetic variations with short wavelengths. The instrument often picks these up as circular magnetic anomalies.

Researchers define the "magnetic signatures" of archaeological features, which helps distinguish cultural remains from

Recording data using a magnetometer near Dunlap Mound. *Photo courtesy Daniel Bigman.*

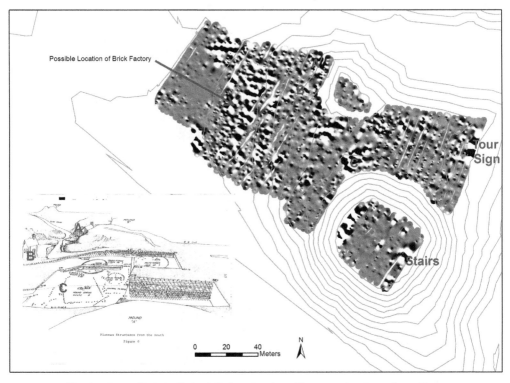

The above images illustrates the type of information gleaned from magnetometer readings of the South Plateau at Ocmulgee. *Graphic by Daniel Bigman.*

modern materials like iron fences or rebar. These modern items produce higher amplitude responses in the magnetometer.

Bigman collected more than two thousand magnetic traces covering an area of more than fifteen hectares (about thirty-seven acres). He processed the data, plotting it to a map and correcting for variations in soil and geology. The remaining magnetic patterns showed either archaeological features underground or later ground disturbance after European contact and settlement.

Electromagnetic Induction (Conductivity)

The electromagnetic conductivity method measures how easy it is to establish an electrical current within buried objects or features. Here's how it works: A portable conductivity meter applies a current to a transmitting coil, then measures the strength of the response from underground. The size, shape, and other properties

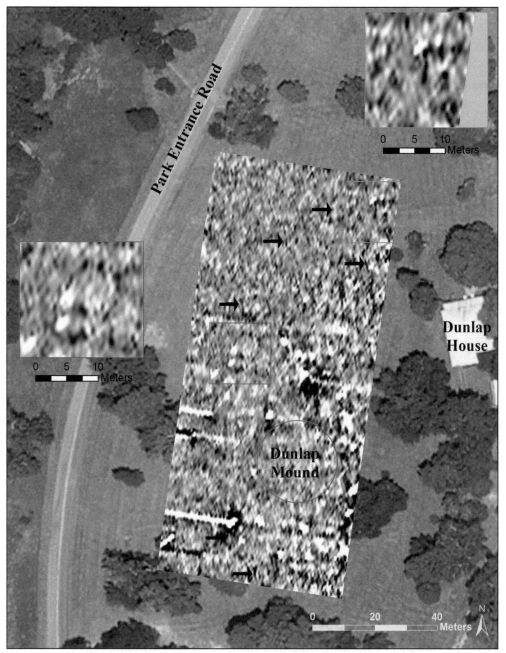

This image shows what is revealed by a conductivity survey of Dunlap Hill. Red and blue inserts show enlargements of two possible Early Mississippian structures. Black arrows indicate additional irregularities that could also be Early Mississippian structures. *Graphic by Daniel Bigman.*

of a buried item determine how well it conducts electricity. The result is compared with surrounding soils.

Archaeological features such as underground postholes or hearths are generally more conductive than background soil. That's because long ago, they were filled in with ash or other organic material that holds more water. A feature like a grave or ditch that was dug out and then filled in with the same soil should conduct less electricity because fill dirt is looser and drains water faster.

Some materials establish an electrical current more easily than others. For example, some metals accept a current immediately. It may take longer to induce a current in a pit of charred wood. By varying the current, conductivity meters can identify different types of materials.

The Ocmulgee survey was designed to locate prehistoric hearths, decayed wooden postholes, burials, and pits. It tested about twenty acres of open land within the historical park.

Ground-penetrating Radar

Ground-penetrating radar (GPR) sends electromagnetic radio waves underground. The speed the wave travels depends on what it's traveling through. Some of the radar wave's energy is reflected back to the surface when it encounters a variation in the energy transfer. The time the reflection takes and the amount of reflection are recorded at the surface by a receiver antenna.

Using GPR technology atop the Great Temple Mound. *Photo courtesy Daniel Bigman.*

GPR Profile from North of Mound C Showing Various Hyperbolic Anomalies

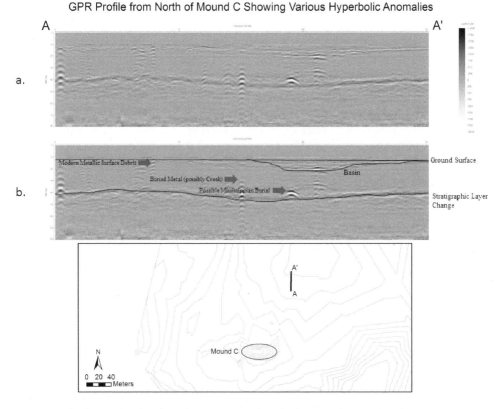

The above images show the 2-dimensional profile based on how ground-penetrating radar waves were reflected from underground at the Funeral Mound (which Bigman refers to as Mound C). Image (a) shows processed data, and (b) is Bigman's interpretation of their meaning. *Graphic by Daniel Bigman.*

The ground-penetrating radar provides a two-dimensional profile of what's underground. A series of these images can be combined to create "horizontal reflection maps," or 3-D images. This process helps archaeologists figure out not only that something is there, but how deep it is buried. Its depth might indicate the time period when it was used.

Bigman collected five survey blocks of ground-penetrating radar results, covering a little more than an acre. These blocks and transects were strategically placed to test several hypotheses about Ocmulgee's physical layout, such as the orientation of the ditch on the northern plateau, the density of possible Mississippian structures on Dunlap Hill, and the extent of the "cemetery" surrounding the Funeral Mound.

Electrical Resistivity

Like electromagnetic induction, the electrical-resistivity technique uses electrical current. However, it uses probes to introduce the current under the ground. The current flows along the path of least resistance. If underground features don't conduct electricity well, the flow of the current will be pushed toward the surface. If the underground area is generally conductive, the current will travel deeper.

A volt meter measures the density of the current at the ground surface. The higher the reading, the more the ground resists the current. A lower reading shows the underground features are more conductive. The flow of the current is affected by the size of spaces between dirt particles and how wet the soil is.

The UGA study restricted the use of electrical resistivity to the ditches at Ocmulgee in an effort to identify the boundaries of the Late Mississippian settlement. The ditches could be expected to represent the edge of the town, but their extent hadn't been determined by previous excavations.

Electrical resistivity field survey equipment in use. *Photo courtesy Daniel Bigman.*

Posthole Tests and
Magnetic Susceptibility

Posthole tests and magnetic-susceptibility tests were used to test possible settlement and occupation outside the ditches, between Mounds X, McDougal, and Dunlap. Bigman wanted to know whether they continued into the woods past the known footprint of the site.

Magnetic susceptibility is a test that measures whether a substance can be magnetized, and by how much. Materials have a magnetic signature that depends on their concentration of magnetic grains, the grain size, and the minerals inside. There are differences between the magnetic signatures of natural soil compared with soil moved or changed by humans. For example, nodules of burnt clay can be identified based on their magnetic properties and grain size. These traces can help researchers find buried landforms and areas where people were active.

At thirty locations, a researcher used a posthole digging tool to remove a shaft of dirt about fifteen centimeters across. This dirt was screened through mesh to find artifacts. Magnetic-susceptibility readings were recorded at base of the "plow zone" within each posthole. (This helped eliminate confusing interference caused by historic farming activity.)

Posthole tests and magnetic-susceptibility readings were often conducted in the woods since ground cover and maneuverability challenges would have made other techniques less accurate there. The only drawback was that loose surface soil and forest debris had to be removed from those spots first. Otherwise, the magnetic-susceptibility test results might be skewed by more recent buildup on the forest floor.

Overall, modern geophysical survey proved an appropriate way to map archaeological features and analyze spatial relationships. The techniques chosen are able to "read" the physical evidence of how people changed the landscape. The next step combined this information with evidence gleaned from the objects people created.

Ceramic Analysis

The second major part of the UGA study focused on analyzing Ocmulgee ceramics found in the past, mostly during Kelly's excavations. The age and location of ceramic fragments were used to draw conclusions about the age of the structures where they were found. The patterns and design of the pottery also reveal clues about what kind of people lived in the buildings and what activities happened there.

The UGA study used a different approach to ceramic analysis from all previous studies. It only analyzed pottery pieces found outside mounds, but it examined every ceramic fragment from each selected excavation site (like a pit or ditch). The study was also the first to sample ceramics from every geographic area at Ocmulgee in a single analysis.

WPA workers excavate a trench at Ocmulgee Mounds. *Photo courtesy National Park Service.*

The site was divided into eight sections. Some were near mounds and others were far from them. For example, the South Plateau contains two mounds while the Middle Plateau has none. The areas included both early and late periods of Early Mississippian occupation and regions of the community with different functions. For instance, the North Plateau contained a residential area while the Funeral Mound Bluff functioned as an Early Mississippian cemetery. (See the map of areas discussed in the text.)

Bigman selected ceramic excavation locations that together would provide maximum coverage of the site and include the most artifacts. In sections that have seen little excavation, such as Dunlap Hill and McDougal Mound Bluff, he tried to analyze the whole ceramic collection.

Ceramic finds discovered during the Works Progress Administration excavations were catalogued on provenience cards. The UGA study searched these cards for each geographic area and recorded key information like the soil layer and depth where each fragment was found.

The study analyzed all the trenches that had been documented with profile drawings and which had complete collections of artifacts at the National Park Service Southeast Archaeological Center. This collection, located in Tallahassee, Florida, stores the majority of the millions of artifacts recovered at Ocmulgee.

In three areas, good information was available about the strata where ceramic artifacts were found: the South Plateau, Middle Plateau (north), and North Plateau. Poor recording or minimal investigations meant that this level of detail was not available for other areas. The Southeast Plateau is severely disturbed, so the excavations recorded there may be less reliable. Nevertheless, the study still used information about the total number of different ceramic types found in these other areas to help reconstruct the community history.

Ceramics were dated and classified using two primary characteristics: surface design and "temper." Temper is the material added to clay to keep it from shrinking or cracking during the process of drying or baking ("firing"). Different temper materials were used at different times and in different regions. At Ocmulgee, temper materials included shell, quartz, and grit composed of a variety of minerals. Each material produces a different finish. Quartz temper can be identified by its angular shape, for example.

The image on the left shows surface differences between Bibb Shell and Bibb Grit temper in Mississippian pottery. The right shows cross-sections of Bibb Shell (top) and Bibb Grit (bottom). *Photos and graphic by Daniel Bigman.*

Sand has a smooth, rounded surface because it has been weathered by water. Occasionally, it also used pottery shapes to help identify the age of items: for example, the shape of a bowl lip or rim, or the form of a cup handle. However, these often couldn't be identified or weren't a consistent enough feature to be helpful.

Bigman sorted pottery pieces by location, temper, and surface treatment. He drew rim profiles to reflect the range of variation in these forms for each ceramic type and took digital photos to document representative specimens for each kind of surface decoration. This multistep classification process allowed him to identify some combinations of temper and surface treatment for the first time.

The UGA study used a diverse set of tools to gather physical evidence about the Early Mississippian settlement at Ocmulgee. Considered comprehensively, these small discoveries display patterns that reveal more about its culture and politics.

CHAPTER 3

A Map in the Ground

Survey Results

The UGA study provides a detailed analysis of what was identified underground by various combinations of survey tools at Ocmulgee Mounds National Historical Park. Previous archaeologists had already subdivided the park into six different zones. However, Bigman adjusted their boundaries to better reflect his interpretation of how the areas relate. The following is a summary of findings from each of the six geographic areas.

WPA workers excavate the temple mounds in 1934. *Photo courtesy of National Park Service.*

The areas discussed in the UGA report on Ocmulgee archaeology. Mound C is commonly called the Funeral Mound. *Graphic by Daniel Bigman.*

South Plateau

The South Plateau contains two major mounds, the Greater and Lesser Temple Mounds. At ninety meters apart, these mounds are closer to each other than any other pair.

The South Plateau and the area to its west have been heavily disturbed. The plateau is south of the two railroad cuts intersecting the park. People lived in the area during the Depression era, as shown by WPA drawings of two houses near the Lesser Temple Mound, and a twentieth-century brick factory may have been located slightly to its west.

Proportionally, Kelly excavated more of the South Plateau than the other main bluffs. The deepest cultural deposits were found there along with a variety of architectural features. Kelly excavated two circular earth lodges/council chambers, each with a fire pit in the center. One appeared to have been rebuilt at least three times. Kelly also found what might have been the remains of residential structures. He collected a mix of pottery from the "floors" of buildings and found evidence that the mounds were built in multiple stages. He also documented features he identified as hearths and two possible crematory fire pits.

The Great Temple Mound was further investigated by National Park Service archaeologists three times in later years, although much of this work was barely documented.

Park Service archaeologist John Walker excavated the South Plateau in 1967 in an attempt to understand the internal structure of the mounds and how they were built. He returned to conduct limited additional testing in 1978. His results from the 1978 investigations were never published, and no adequate account has been written about his work and methods.

The most recent investigation on the South Plateau took the form of shovel tests in 2000, when the Park Service was considering adding a new sidewalk and steps. The area around the base of the Great Temple Mound was found to be heavily disturbed, exhibiting a mixture of Mississippian and historic artifacts and many types of soil jumbled together.

The review of previous research revealed several unanswered questions about the form and function of the Great Temple Mound as well as the timeline of its construction. For example, there seem

A family looks from the stairs of the Great Temple Mound across a wetland toward the Ocmulgee River. *Photo by Sharman Ayoub.*

to be contradictory interpretations about whether steps were used along with ramps at the corners of the mound.

Another problem emerges in the contrasting accounts of architecture on top of the mound. Kelly identified a single feature on the mound summit in the 1930s, but Walker identified a fire pit and several post molds. It's unclear whether these contradictory observations came from the same layer, or if the features Walker found were in a deeper layer. The fragmented evidence from the summit of the mound might also have been caused by destructive plowing.

Although all archaeologists identified a clay cap on the mound, only the WPA investigations found more than one. It does seem clear that the mound went through multiple phases of construction over the course of its history.

The new UGA investigations used magnetometry to survey a broad swath of the South Plateau. However, the effort provided little new insight into the Mississippian period. Bigman also used conductivity and ground-penetrating radar at the summit of the

Great Temple Mound to learn more about how it was built. None of these techniques found evidence of structures on top of the final cap of the Great Temple Mound.

Two-dimensional profile views of the mound, created using ground-penetrating radar, showed the mound had at least four clay caps. These results also showed that the mound had expanded westward to its maximum horizontal extent for the final three phases that it was used.

Patterns beneath the later clay caps indicate that earlier versions of the mound likely had buildings on top. The size, location, orientation, and style of these structural elements evolved through time. This suggests that the Great Temple Mound served different functions for the community over the years.

Middle Plateau

The Middle Plateau area is located between the North and South Plateaus and is separated from each by a railroad cut. One of these old railbeds is now covered with concrete and used as a tour road to reach the South Plateau and the Funeral Mound. Trains still run on the other. A marshy area separates the Middle Plateau from the Funeral Mound.

A train's head lamp cuts through the darkness as it traverses Ocmulgee Mounds National Historical Park. *Photo by Sharman Ayoub.*

The Middle Plateau is disturbed by a bridge, a narrow side-walk, and plowing. In addition, the remains of a historic Creek town dating to about 1680 are found here. The Creek town makes it tough to pin a date on underground features identified through geophysical surveys.

Kelly's excavations of the Middle Plateau found up to ten possible structures. Some weren't well-documented. Through the years, archaeologists have disagreed on whether some dated to the prehistoric period or the era when the area hosted a trading post between Europeans and American Indians.

Bigman surveyed this area using magnetometer and con-ductivity testing. His goal was to measure the general density of occupation and map the distribution of square and round structures. He found many magnetic anomalies representing archaeological features and interpreted this to indicate the Middle Plateau had been densely populated. These might have dated mostly to the Creek occupation, because no features could be confidently identified as the kind of square structures used in Mississippian architecture. Still, Bigman considers it likely that at least a portion of the magnetic anomalies probably date to the Early Mississippian period.

There was a lot of variability in the conductivity results for the area, which indicates it was densely occupied for a long time. Individual structures may be hard to identify in a reoccupied area with many residents because overlap of building and rebuilding creates abrupt variations in the density of the soil and its content. Although this creates "messy" data, it helps archaeologists draw conclusions about how people were using the broader landscape, and for how long. The UGA conductivity results support the idea that the Middle Plateau was part of a continuously inhabited zone during the Early Mississippian period.

The UGA study did reveal some specifics about buildings on the Middle Plateau: magnetic results could be interpreted as several round or oval structures, similar to those found by Kelly nearby.

The excavation, conductivity, and magnetic tests suggest that Early Mississippians lived in a broad occupation zone from the South Plateau, across the Middle Plateau, to the North Plateau. This new evidence challenges the idea that a subcommunity lived on the main bluff. However, conductivity results, combined with

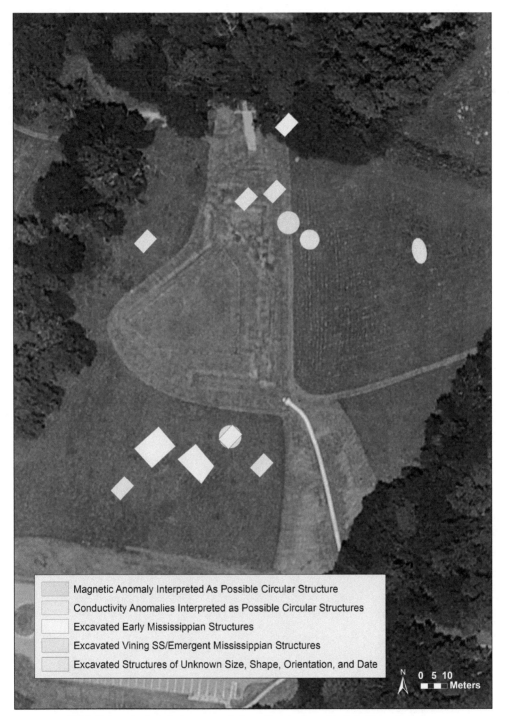

Middle Plateau structures that were excavated as well as structures detected with geophysical detection methods. *Graphic by Daniel Bigman.*

ceramic artifacts, indicate that people occupied the Southeast Plateau approximately four thousand years ago—since the Late Archaic period—much earlier than on the Middle Plateau.

North Plateau

The North Plateau is the upland area north of both railroad cuts. It's bordered by Walnut Creek and its tributary. This plateau's most famous features are the Earth Lodge and the Cornfield Mound.

Although the South Plateau received the greatest attention in proportion to its size, Kelly excavated more area of the North Plateau than any other segment. WPA workers unearthed many buildings, irregular posthole patterns, and clay floors there. Kelly found evidence of two earth lodges, thirty-eight burials (including several slave burials), and more than 220 pits. This area was referred to as the Stratified Village Site because of the high number of postholes and pits found at different depths. Kelly uncovered several structures that might have been homes.

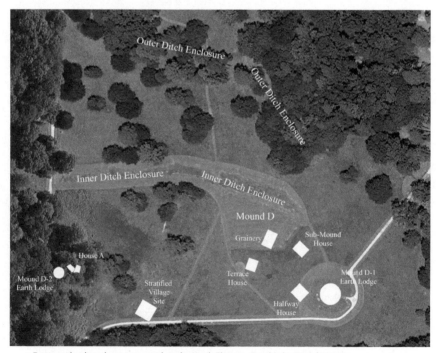

Features that have been excavated on the North Plateau. *Graphic by Daniel Bigman.*

Despite the size of WPA excavations, they didn't clarify the extent of the area where people lived. Many of the excavation trenches were widely spaced, and a large area was left uninvestigated immediately south and west of the Cornfield Mound. Filling this gap in the data is critical for testing the idea that the settlement was divided into subcommunities.

Bigman's geophysical survey recorded anomalies consistent with expectations for buildings with many internal pits, which didn't happen much elsewhere at Ocmulgee during the Early Mississippian era. This suggests people living on the North Plateau accumulated more goods or food. Or it could indicate the North Plateau was used for a specialized function. Although archaeologists Mark Williams and Joseph Henderson described the contents of the pits—presumably from Kelly's notes on the excavations—neither they nor Bigman could locate the actual artifacts.

Kelly found two long, prehistoric trenches that extend across the North, Middle, and South Plateaus. (See map.) Archaeologists have since proposed that they were built primarily for defense but might have also been used to separate space and control pedestrian traffic. The excavated dirt might have been used to build houses.

Depression-era excavation work at Ocmulgee found many structures and artifacts. But the spacing of its trenches and recording of its findings were less systematic than modern archaeological projects. *Photo courtesy of National Park Service.*

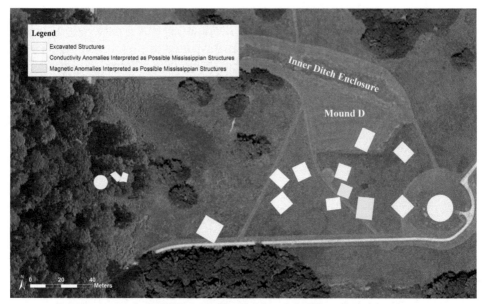

These structures on the North Plateau were identified through the UGA geophysical detection survey as well as excavation. *Graphic by Daniel Bigman.*

Similar multifunctional ditch and wall enclosures have been observed at Etowah, another Early Mississippian settlement in Georgia.

Bigman found that these trenches extend west beyond the area excavated in the 1930s. This suggests that people lived on the entire main bluff enclosed by the ditch. Magnetometer readings found little evidence that people lived in the area between the two ditches.

UGA conductivity and magnetic surveys found evidence of people living west and south of the Cornfield Mound. For example, Bigman identified four anomalies he interprets as possible structures with a small circular variation between them. This suggests a possible residential courtyard group or household cluster. Similar arrangements of houses have been found at other Early Mississippian sites such as Etowah and Moundville.

The total field magnetic data also indicate that people might have lived more densely on the North Plateau than the WPA findings suggested. Again, these conclusions challenge the idea that the main bluff at Ocmulgee was a subcommunity. Instead, they support the alternative view that the settlement functioned as a single, larger community.

Funeral Mound Bluff

The Funeral Mound is on a bluff on the southwestern corner of Ocmulgee Mounds National Historical Park. It was named for the many burials within the mound and surrounding areas. The mound is separated from the Middle Plateau by a marshy area. The bluff continues north of the Cornfield Mound into Drake's Field. Once a series of Little League baseball fields, Drake's Field was donated to the park in 1991. It is separated from the Funeral Mound by the Central of Georgia Railroad's tracks, the construction of which destroyed a large part of the northern side of the Funeral Mound. A fence at the edge of Drake's Field separates the park from the adjacent Fort Hill neighborhood.

Kelly's excavations in this part of the park were focused on the mound. The National Park Service also conducted some archaeological work west and north of it. Almost all the artifacts recovered were Creek. While possible buried structures were identified during the UGA survey, those were probably built by the historic Creek community.

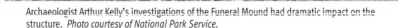

Archaeologist Arthur Kelly's investigations of the Funeral Mound had dramatic impact on the structure. *Photo courtesy of National Park Service.*

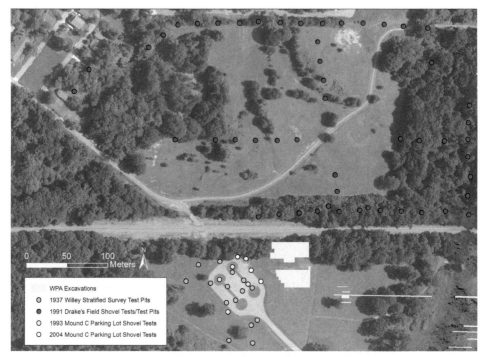

The history of excavation test pits in the Funeral Mound. *Graphic by Daniel Bigman.*

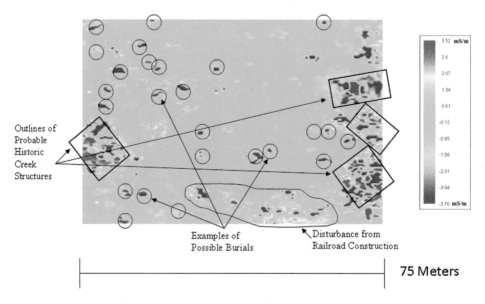

Features revealed by conductivity testing in a survey block at the Funeral Mound.
Graphic by Daniel Bigman.

The Funeral Mound marks the western boundary of the Early Mississippian community. The UGA geophysical survey confirmed that the area around the mound was used as a cemetery, and no one lived there. The Funeral Mound Bluff probably served only ritual purposes.

Results from conductivity tests and ground-penetrating radar suggest the cemetery extends north and east of the mound; many of the burials might be from the Creek era (roughly 1620–1820). The UGA investigations found more than sixty anomalies consistent with Native American burials, revealing that the cemetery was denser and larger than previously known.

The Early Mississippian population was estimated to be much larger than the number of Funeral Mound burials from that period. This suggests that only a select group of people had the right to be buried around the Funeral Mound. The elaborate goods buried with some individuals suggest that this cemetery was reserved for wealthy or powerful people, a theory reinforced by another finding: although WPA excavations found many Early Mississippian burials in the Middle and North Plateaus, log tombs were found only beneath the Funeral Mound.

Mound X Ridge and Northern Lowlands

The Mound X ridge is located north of the outer ditch, next to the Northern Plateau and surrounded by the Northern Lowlands.

Kelly excavated trenches on the mound's ridge during the 1930s but paid less attention to this area than other parts of the main bluff. The mound wasn't identified by Kelly; in fact, it was first recognized by Mark Williams and Joseph Henderson in 1974 from a profile drawing, backed up by a couple of historical references. It was designated Mound X because of the "tentative nature of its existence." Mound X and the surrounding area have never been accurately dated. Kelly lumped this area in with the North Plateau.

The Northern Lowlands were investigated just once, very minimally, in 1978. The findings of archaeologist John Walker suggest that no one lived in the area during the Early Mississippian period.

The UGA study used magnetic-susceptibility and posthole testing to search for a neighborhood around Mound X or any evidence of Early Mississippians living between it and Dunlap or McDougal Mounds.

Bigman recovered artifacts from his posthole tests in this section of the park. Three of eight recovered pottery fragments are probably from the Early Mississippian period. Other artifacts recovered include flint flakes from making tools or weapons, fired clay, and red ochre, along with ground stone colored by red pigment. Both posthole tests and magnetic test results helped Bigman conclude that the Early Mississippian community didn't extend north beyond the modern park road.

Magnetometer testing found anomalies that represent hearths, pits, clusters of artifacts, or other features. Most are closer to Mound X than to the outer ditch, which suggests that the mound was the center of a small neighborhood separate from the main settlement.

Dunlap Hill and Dunlap Mound

Dunlap Hill is a bluff located in the northeastern section of the park that was named for Samuel Dunlap, the head of the family that owned the land for most of the 1800s. The Dunlap House— the centerpiece of a dairy farm and cotton plantation—remains a historic landmark on the bluff. Dunlap Mound is also located on the bluff and marks the highest point in the study area. On the southern edge of Dunlap Hill is the park visitor center.

The area has been heavily used ever since the Mississippian era; not only was it part of a farm, but a Civil War defensive earthwork was built by the Union in the southeast corner. Many buildings, such as barns and servants' quarters, were built on the land even after the Civil War. Their locations have been documented by historic maps as well as archaeological surveys. More recently, a portion of the study area has been used for parking during the park's annual Ocmulgee Indigenous Celebration, which draws upwards of fifteen thousand visitors a year.

WPA excavations concentrated on Dunlap Mound. Kelly found evidence that a rectangular structure topped the original mound. During investigations on Dunlap Hill (but not the mound) between 1978 and 2006, the National Park Service recovered plain ceramic artifacts from the Early Mississippian period, which suggests Dunlap Hill was a residential area during that time. But the scarcity of buildings also suggests that this occupation might have been brief.

Archaeologists work on the McDougal and Dunlap mounds in 1936.
Photo courtesy of National Park Service.

The activity on Dunlap Hill over many centuries creates lots of "noise" for the archeologist hunting Early Mississippian evidence. Nonetheless, the UGA study collected useful information about native buildings, where they were located, and the size of the settlement.

The magnetometer identified one large circular anomaly directly west of Dunlap Mound. Several anomalies representing pits, hearths, or large postholes were located inside the border of this circle. It would be speculative to say this represents an earth lodge or council chamber, but its size, shape, and the composition of its features are similar to earth lodges uncovered by Kelly on the North and South Plateaus.

Geophysical survey results indicate that households were concentrated near the Dunlap Mound. (The UGA survey was the first to identify structures near the mound.) Artifacts show activities also took place outside the homesites.

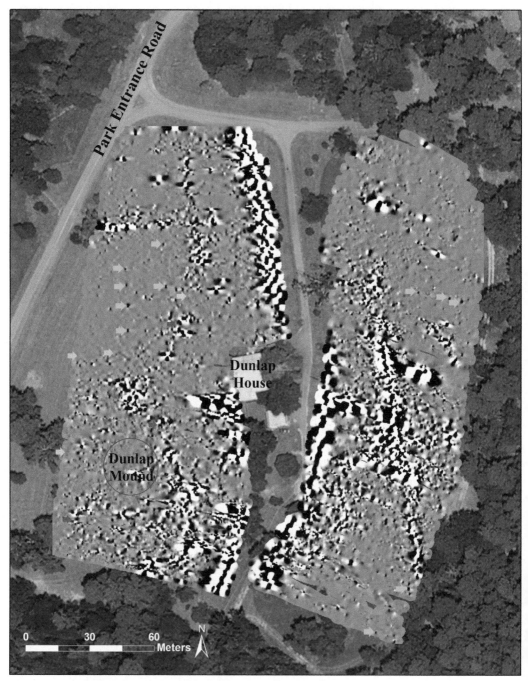

Total field magnetic data from Dunlap Hill. Red arrows indicate locations of possible burned structures, orange arrows indicate possible unburned structures, and green arrows indicate small positive magnetic anomalies representative of hearths or pits. *Graphic by Daniel Bigman.*

There is a clear open space between this neighborhood and the North Plateau. The Dunlap Hill settlement was isolated from the rest of the town and from other neighborhoods. This supports a claim by previous researchers that Dunlap Mound was the nucleus of a subcommunity.

Ceramic Chronology

Pottery types are often used to identify when people used particular areas and when buildings were constructed, so it's important to understand when different ceramic techniques and decorations were invented and used. If these markers are placed incorrectly, then conclusions about the timing of human settlements will also be incorrect.

Examples of Vining simple stamped pottery. *Photo by Daniel Bigman.*

GENERAL CERAMIC DECORATION TYPES BY PERIOD

Swift Creek (500–750 A.D.): sand-tempered, complicated stamped-pottery style named for a nearby archaeological site at an Ocmulgee tributary called Swift Creek.

Napier Complicated Stamped and **Woodstock Complicated Stamped** (750/800–1020 A.D.): detailed, complicated stamped designs appearing with many variations of parallel linear stamping, curved stamping, diamonds, nested diamonds, and sometimes combinations of these together or appearing with other slight variations.

Vining Simple Stamped (800–1200 A.D.): a quartz-tempered ware with linear impressions.

Etowah Complicated Stamped (1000–1200 A.D.): recognized by "ladder base diamond" and "line block stamp" motifs, although these evolve over time.

Savannah Complicated Stamped (After 1200 A.D.): concentric circles.

Swift Creek

Napier Complicated

Woodstock Complicated

Vining Simple

Etowah Complicated

Savannah Complicated

Photos courtesy of Peach State Archaeological Society / University of Georgia and Florida Museum / University of Florida

Before the UGA study, the timing of Ocmulgee settlement hadn't been reexamined for about forty years. In the intervening decades, researchers have revised their estimate of when the Vining Simple Stamped ceramic pattern came into use. It had been dated to the Early Woodland period, but since the 1990s, archaeologists revised its timeline to the period from 800 a.d. to 1200 a.d. This later timeframe makes it a useful indicator of Early Mississippian settlement.

A leading reconstruction of Ocmulgee community history was based on the idea that Bibb Plain ceramics were made with less and less shell material over time. But that concept was developed through analysis of only two mounds sites and a single occupational site. The UGA study incorporated data from more sites to solidify this interpretation.

The UGA ceramic analysis had three goals:

(1) To evaluate whether shell-tempered and Vining Simple Stamped pottery were created and used during the same time period;

(2) To test previous observations that the use of shell declined during the Early Mississippian period; and

(3) To refine the ceramic chronology by comparing other characteristics such as lip mode, handle form, decoration, and surface treatment.

Bigman classified ceramics unearthed at Ocmulgee based mostly on their surface decorations (such as stamping) and temper material (such as shell, grit, quartz, or sand). Variations in ceramic types and the shape of bowl and plate "lips" were tracked through time. The names of different ceramic types sometimes vary only slightly to distinguish different types of decoration. (Examples are Vining Simple Stamped, Vining Complicated Stamped, and Vining Plain.)

Bigman provided a deeper analysis of variations he found within a single broad category of tempering: the Bibb Plain type. He developed his chronology by tracking where ceramics were found within soil layers of three different Ocmulgee settlement areas: the North Plateau, the Middle Plateau (north), and the South Plateau.

As a result of his analysis, Bigman proposed four chronological stages in the ceramic deposits. (See box.)

Examples of Bibb plain ceramics. *Photo by Daniel Bigman.*

The study reached a few other key conclusions about Ocmulgee ceramics. It found that the Vining Simple Stamped pattern was
more abundant in early layers but continued through time. Bibb
Shell was found more frequently in deeper layers representing
earlier eras, and this study confirmed that it was used less as time
went by. The lips of ceramic vessels had similar shapes in earlier
periods, but they developed more variety over the years. In the
most recent layer, they simplified again.

Bigman noted a limitation in his analysis: he couldn't classify
the Vining Plain pottery type because Vining forms and temper
were not well-defined at Ocmulgee before his study. His work clar-
ified these features somewhat, but he grouped possible Vining
Plain in the same category with other plain grit ceramics. The

study urges future researchers to classify Vining Plain. Knowing when it was used could refine the interpretation of Ocmulgee settlement history.

Overall, the UGA survey used a greater variety and combination of tools and methods to investigate the Ocmulgee Mounds site than previous studies. These located new underground evidence of potentially significant structures. Bigman also proposed a major change in ceramic chronology, with far-reaching impacts for understanding the settlement. The UGA findings reveal more pieces of a puzzle that, fit together, show where and when activities occurred in the community. We are provided with a clearer picture of the rise and fall of elite leadership structures as well as how residential groups interacted.

Photo by Sharman Ayoub.

CHAPTER 4

A Community through Time

Findings

By reconstructing site settlement histories, archaeologists can compare how different mound-associated towns developed. Such detailed histories have been reconstructed for other large, multi-mound Mississippian centers such as Moundville, Cahokia, Etowah, and Lake George. But Ocmulgee had been neglected in this respect. This UGA analysis provides a timeline of Ocmulgee settlement so its emergence, leadership, and historical sequence can be compared to other large mound towns. This helps us understand broad similarities and differences across the Mississippian world.

The UGA study concluded that the Early Mississippian Ocmulgee settlement was built and inhabited in five stages. Each stage shows how the changing physical layout reflected changes in how people in the community related to each other. In reality, these stages weren't distinct, but rather flowed into one another as the community continuously evolved.

To create this timeline, the study compared the frequencies of different ceramic types (representing different time periods) across the site. Especially important to this understanding was the ratio of Vining Simple Stamped pottery (as a marker of early settlement) to Bibb Grit (a marker of later settlement).

When it comes to understanding power relationships and status, the key ceramic indicator proved to be Halstead Plain pottery. It was rare but found near public architecture. This seems to indicate that it was prized. Its use decreased over time, but it was mostly associated with mounds.

Another, although smaller, factor in chronology had to do with the different types of rims found on ceramic fragments. Square, flattened, or rounded lips were popular at different times and help date the landscape features where they are found. Their number and diversity in different areas of the Ocmulgee settlement provide supporting clues about when people began living there and for how long.

Geophysical testing and some limited excavation also helped with reconstructing the settlement layout. Based on the evolving town landscape, Bigman developed theories about power relationships and social inequality.

The UGA study found that the southern portion of Ocmulgee was occupied first. The settlement then expanded east and west, covering the Funeral Mound area and the Southeast Plateau. As the population grew, it spread to the northern portion of the Middle Plateau and the North Plateau. The last places people

The Lesser Temple Mound covered with morning frost. *Photo by Sharman Ayoub.*

settled were Dunlap Hill and presumably the other northern bluffs where McDougal Mound and Fort Hawkins are located.

It's unclear whether people lived on the outer bluffs at the same time as on the main bluff during an overlapping period or only after the main bluff was abandoned. Bigman suspected McDougal Mound and the Fort Hawkins area were occupied at the same time as Dunlap Hill since no Vining Simple Stamped pottery was recovered from either. But he did not reach a firm conclusion because so little evidence was recovered near the McDougal Mound and Fort Hawkins.

Stage 1: Origins

Social inequality was minimal during the first stage of the Mississippian settlement at Ocmulgee. Although there might have been leaders, power was probably distributed among household groups.

The people who lived at Ocmulgee during the first stage of settlement probably constructed round homes using a single "set post" technique. Kelly found examples of this architecture only on the Middle and South Plateaus, the earliest occupied areas. The houses excavated there during the 1930s were between 4.5 and 10 meters wide, and some had fire pits. The UGA study identified three more buried features that Bigman interpreted as round

A recreated example of a wattle-and-daub type of house. *Courtesy of National Park Service.*

structures presumably dating to the same time. One had an anomaly, found by conductivity testing, that might indicate a fire pit.

The layout of the Stage 1 community is difficult to reconstruct with the available information. There is considerable distance between houses—both those that were excavated and those that are indicated by ground-sensing tests. But it's likely that anything built in between them might have been destroyed later by the railroad and park road. Plus, construction of the 1680 trading post on the Middle Plateau might have damaged the remains of some buildings.

The Stage 1 wooden structures seem to be found clustered in groups as well as by themselves. This implies that some households lived in a single building while others used some kind of compound. The long history of occupation makes it hard to be sure whether the household clusters were separated by open space. This survey couldn't detect a larger community layout, such as a circular grouping around a community-wide plaza.

A view of the Funeral Mound from the temple mounds. *Photo by Sharman Ayoub.*

Neither the UGA survey nor previous investigations found buildings on the Funeral Mound. The Funeral Mound Bluff was being used by the community in this stage, before a mound was ever built there. Postholes and pits under layers of soil within the mound may indicate a structure there that preceded the mound. The few pottery fragments found there led Bigman to date this structure to Stage 1. He suggested these remains probably weren't part of a house where people lived because the Funeral Mound seems to have always been used for specialized functions.

The Funeral Mound bluff was higher in elevation than the settlement on the main bluff and probably could have been seen by the entire community at all times. This might have promoted an integrated sense of community. Social inequality between residential groups was uncommon, and political leaders had little influence.

Stage 2: Transformation

The second stage saw important changes to the social and physical landscape of Ocmulgee. The size of the settlement increased slightly, expanding east to include the Southeast Plateau. People might not have lived on the Southeast Plateau during the early part of Stage 2 (see area map), but instead might have used it for specialized work. Bigman suggests it might have been a pottery workshop producing large Hawkins Fabric Marked circular basins, or a place where people conducted some other activity that required large basins.

The Middle Plateau might not have been very densely occupied at the beginning of this stage, but the population increased over time. Construction began on the Greater and Lesser Temple

Examples of Hawkins fabric marked pottery. *Photo by Daniel Bigman.*

An imagined "slice of life" in a Mississippian town. *Courtesy of National Park Service.*

Mounds and the Funeral Mound, and access to them was probably restricted. The community also began building the South Plateau earth lodges.

Homes transitioned from a circular to square shape during the second stage of occupation. WPA and Park Service excavations and the UGA geophysical survey recorded more square buildings than circular ones inside the town's footprint during this stage.

People lived in household clusters. These contained more buildings and might have been closer together than homes built during the first stage. The household clusters surrounded open space on two or three sides but didn't fully enclose courtyards. Expansion of these compounds might have overlapped into Stage 3. It's hard to tell which buildings were used during each stage, but the first expansions probably happened quickly. There is evidence of rebuilding and wall refurbishment, which reflects a personal attachment to a home place.

The UGA study identified only three or four household clusters. However, magnetic and conductivity tests suggest the entire Middle Plateau was filled with architecture. Identifiable buildings account for only a fraction of the total structures being used during this expansion period. The remains of many buildings were probably destroyed by later plowing and erosion.

The South Plateau began to extend west during Stage 2. Evidence suggests that the Great Temple Mound was a considerable size and needed a larger foundation to support its growing mass by the end of this stage. There also appear to be more square buildings added on the extended bluff, housing a growing population

The UGA survey identified possible structures on top of the Great Temple Mound from early in its construction. The earliest of these could be interpreted as a "paired" structure. Archaeologists have identified possible paired structures on Mississippian mounds at other settlements, such as Obion, Hiwassee Island, Cemochechobee, and Kincaid. This kind of building could reflect that a chief or centralized political leader had emerged by the end of Stage 2.

There were other signs of emerging centralized leadership and increasing social inequality. The largest square house, two earth lodges, and a specialized structure only seen on the South Plateau were all built close to the Great Temple Mound. The mound was probably only accessible to an exclusive group.

In addition, more Halstead pottery was found on the South Plateau and the Funeral Mound bluff, showing that the people who lived or worked in these areas had access to precious items.

Mound building suggests leaders began to exercise power and influence over the general population. Funeral Mound construction began during this second stage. This mound contains more construction layers than others at Ocmulgee, showing it was used for an extended period—possibly until the whole settlement was abandoned. The mound was built over a spot that seems to have always been kept separate from community living space. Access to the Funeral Mound was probably limited. The number of elite burials associated with it increased over time.

Stage 3: Expansion

The size of the town grew dramatically during the third phase to include the North Plateau. Along with the Middle Plateau, the new part of town became densely populated.

An Aerial view of the Ocmulgee Mounds National Historical Park. *Photo by Sharman Ayoub.*

The Cornfield Mound complex (see map) on the North Plateau was built during this stage. Homes grouped in courtyards close to the Cornfield Mound and the nearby earth lodge are constructed more formally, with fully enclosed courtyards. This layout contrasted with the household clusters on the Middle Plateau. Those were assembled less formally and not enclosed on all sides. This might have encouraged social interaction between household groups. The variation in architecture seems to indicate an emerging elite class vying for power.

It might also reflect growing political tension: people living on the Cornfield Mound and in nearby courtyards might have challenged the traditional power structure, which had been monopolized by those living near the Great Temple Mound.

During the third stage, social inequality reached its peak. Not only were some people not allowed access to fine goods and public architecture, but the elite began to hide those things from view in their enclosed courtyards.

During this stage, Ocmulgee's occupants excavated the outer ditch (see map) enclosing the North, Middle, and South Plateaus. To carry out this large public works project, as well as continued mound-building, political leaders had to demonstrate enough authority to mobilize labor and plan community-wide activities.

Stage 4: Social and geographic shift

Fewer people lived on the main bluff during Stage 4. Instead, the outlying bluffs housed more people. Those new neighborhoods could have been settled by migrants, the overflow of a growing population, residents who moved away from the main bluff—or some combination of these.

People stopped living near the Greater and Lesser Temple Mounds and the South Plateau. Mound X and the Southeast Mound were constructed on the boundaries of the main bluff outside the ditch. Dunlap Mound, McDougal Mound, and possibly the Fort Hawkins mounds were constructed on the northern bluffs, with empty space between them. (See area map.) This was a change from the traditional layout style on the main bluff, which featured one continuous residential zone.

The new outlying bluff neighborhoods were different. Houses were arranged in a circle around a small mound, which might have played an important role in neighborhood ceremonies. All residents seem to have had access to their neighborhood mound. This shows a more distributed power structure within residential clusters. New leaders probably emerged in these freshly constructed neighborhoods. Changes in the layout of individual mound neighborhoods also demonstrated more social equality among neighborhoods. Bigman concludes that during this stage, power was shared among up to seven residential mound groups (including Fort Hawkins, outside the modern park).

An inner ditch was built during Stage 4. It enclosed a smaller area, including the North and Middle Plateaus. The Great Temple Mound complex was outside this ditch. A final clay cap was laid on the Great Temple Mound.

Stage 5: Dwindling Population and Abandonment

During the final stage, the number of residents at Ocmulgee plummeted and its inhabited area shrank dramatically. Either a small population remained or the area was briefly abandoned and then resettled by a small group. The remaining residents moved south of the main bluff to Ocmulgee Bottoms and stopped using the mounds altogether.

It is clear that Ocmulgee's power and influence diminished on a larger regional scale. At the same time, Etowah's influence began to increase across Georgia.

Bigman could gather little about social inequality or political influence during the final period in which people lived at Ocmulgee. He speculated that social hierarchy and strong central leadership continued to fade. Few inhabitants, if any, remained at Ocmulgee by the Middle Mississippian phase, locally known as the Lamar period (about 1350–1600).

Comparison to Other Mississippian Towns

The UGA study compared Ocmulgee's historical development to what we know of two other large Early Mississippian towns. Like Ocmulgee, Moundville in modern Alabama and Etowah in North Georgia all started small, without mounds.

The earliest evidence of occupation at Moundville began around 1050 a.d. Surrounding settlers in the Black Warrior River Valley lived in small farmsteads, but Moundville supported a denser population that constructed two mounds. Similarly, Etowah consisted of homes and non-mound public architecture during its earliest phase of occupation.

The towns might have arisen under similar conditions—no different from many other villages of the time that did not become prominent. For example, people might have initially chosen the town locations for river access or rich floodplain soils. The settlements don't appear to have been preconceived as regional capitals. That kind of planning and social contract among regional communities appears unlikely from the available evidence.

Etowah Indian Mounds outside Etowah, Georgia. *Courtesy of Georgia State Parks.*

Once the Mississippian settlements were founded, Etowah seems to have seen more rapid population growth than the other two. Moundville didn't expand until about 150 years after it was founded. Unfortunately, settlement and expansion dates are less clear for Ocmulgee.

Ocmulgee seems to have developed a more conspicuous two-tiered hierarchy than the other two towns. The divide between social groups is visible in many physical ways: the distance between different households and mounds; the larger sizes of homes close to mounds and earth lodges; the limited number of elaborate burials at the Funeral Mound; and the higher frequency of precious items near mounds, earth lodges, and large houses.

Moundville and Etowah seem to be similar to each other in their development. The difference between the two is magnitude. Moundville witnessed an explosion of mound construction, and residential clusters became associated with mound pairs.

Unoccupied space separated each pair of mounds and their associated homes. Building sizes varied within the residential clusters,
but there didn't tend to be neighborhoods where all the buildings
were bigger than in other neighborhoods. This might indicate
power-sharing relationships.

Similarly, the town plan of early Etowah used neighborhood
groupings of houses around large courtyards. No clear leadership hierarchy existed. However, in Etowah's growth period there
were differences in the sizes of courtyard groups, and construction
might have begun on several mounds. This might indicate that
Etowah had a power-sharing government with a loose hierarchy.

Unlike Ocmulgee and Moundville, which were occupied continuously throughout their histories, Etowah was abandoned for
a while after its initial expansion. This could have been the result
of cycling through chieftains.

However, a difference between Ocmulgee and Moundville is
the length of time they were occupied. Moundville lasted four

Sun sets beyond the temple mounds in fall. *Photo by Sharman Ayoub.*

hundred to five hundred years while Ocmulgee might have been populated only for one or two centuries. It appears to have seen limited rebuilding. This question might be better resolved through future ceramic studies coupled with new radio-carbon dating.

During the next phase of occupation, Etowah and Moundville share a similar history while Ocmulgee diverges. In the other two towns, leaders began to monopolize power. Based on the number of homes, town populations seemed to have decreased, but construction of monumental public architecture continued. Leaders were distancing themselves from their constituents while drawing on labor from outlying areas.

Ocmulgee, on the other hand, might have seen the development of a political rivalry as the Cornfield Mound complex was built. Bigman concludes from his research that a power struggle was unfolding within the Ocmulgee community even as Moundville and Etowah leaders were solidifying their monopoly on power. When Ocmulgee's residents moved away from the main bluff and stopped using its mounds, the general public seemed to gain more access to public architecture.

Finally, Ocmulgee and Moundville share a common demise. Mound construction stopped and small residual populations remained. Residents clustered into a small, confined space in the southern portions of the towns.

Etowah died a more sudden death. Evidence suggests it was attacked and suffered a devastating defeat. For example, archeological and geophysical evidence shows that the enormous palisade wall was burned. A third reoccupation of Etowah occurred in the later Mississippian, when it might have been home to another community that was part of a larger political system.

Etowah's evolution was typical of "chiefdom cycling." Moundville and Ocmulgee, on the other hand, were unusual in that they witnessed the kind of dramatic changes in elite power and social inequality that are typical of precarious chiefdoms—but *without* cycles of abandonment and reoccupation. Instead, their populations shifted and restructured.

This comparison illustrates the varied lives of Mississippian towns and political systems. Despite their similar cultures, their diverging histories potentially reflect very different local pressures.

Ocmulgee in Wider Context

The UGA study went on to use regional data to analyze the prehistoric social and political landscape. Ocmulgee was compared with other sites around the region containing Late Mississippian ceramics. First, sites within twenty kilometers (around twelve miles) were included. Then the scope expanded to fifty kilometers (about thirty-one miles).

Ceramic artifacts provide clues about how people might have moved around regionally. Two other separate population clusters were found this way, indicating significant settlements. The data led Bigman to suggest that Ocmulgee might have integrated people as far as fifty kilometers away from the central mounds.

Bigman developed new theories about the role local people played in the rise of Ocmulgee. Using previous interpretations of when different ceramic styles were used, other archaeologists argued that Ocmulgee was created by a mass migration from outside the region. However, the revised UGA chronology Bigman developed suggests that Ocmulgee evolved from the local population and was built by native residents.

Bigman suggests that future research could explore Ocmulgee's development in more detail, particularly in relation to its regional neighbors. Interesting questions remain unanswered: What relationship did Ocmulgee have with nearby Brown's Mount (which also has a mound and structures from the Mississippian era)? Did Ocmulgee choose to isolate itself from the rest of the subregion? Or did other towns place a taboo on the community's new ceremonial, political, or social practices? Did Ocmulgee have a connection to the Cahokia civilization whose remains are found in modern-day Illinois?

For a significant era just before Europeans arrived, the Mississippian culture flourished over a wide expanse of North America. After appearing in the Mississippi River Valley, this culture spread regionally in all directions from roughly A.D. 800 to 1600. The Mississippians were more than a single tribe; they were an interconnected civilization that developed in what is now the Midwestern, Eastern, and Southeastern United States. Their society was marked by politically stratified cities and towns, based around farming and building great earthworks. Remnants of this culture can be found in sites stretching from Wisconsin to Oklahoma to the Gulf Coast. Ocmulgee represents one of the Southeastern-most bastions of this culture and the emergence of a settled, large-scale agricultural society.

This UGA study provides new insights into Ocmulgee's growth and development as a Mississippian cultural center as well as its position within the larger Mississippian world. Further, it provides a window into the social and political development of a culture that established Ocmulgee as a crossroads of regional trade, transportation, and political power until the present day.

The National Trust for Historic Preservation has identified Ocmulgee as one of the nation's richest archaeological landscapes. Undiscovered and little-investigated archaeological sites related to Ocmulgee remain scattered up and down the Ocmulgee River and throughout Middle Georgia. Much remains to be learned. However, this study has provided detailed site analyses and broader regional context that lay the groundwork for future research on Ocmulgee's part in the evolution of human civilization in North America.

Photo by Sharman Ayoub.

References

Archaeology of the Moundville Chiefdom. Edited by Vernon J. Knight Jr. and Vincas P. Steponaitis. Washington, DC: Smithsonian Institution Press, 1998.

Bigman, Daniel P. "An Early Mississippian Settlement History of Ocmulgee." PhD diss., Department of Anthropology, University of Georgia, Athens, 2012.

———. "Mapping Plow Zone Soil Magnetism to Delineate Disturbed Archaeological Site Boundaries." *Journal of Archaeological Sciences* 42 (2014): 367–72. doi.org/10.1016/j.jas.2013.11.022

Bigman, Daniel P., Adam King, and Chester Walker. "Geophysical Investigations and New Interpretations of Etowah's Palisade." *Southeastern Archaeology* 30 (2011): 38–50.

Bigman, Daniel P. and Peter M. Lanzarone. "Investigating Construction History, Labor Investment, and Social Change at Ocmulgee National Monument's Mound A, Georgia, USA, Using Ground Penetrating Radar." *Archaeological Prospection* (March 12, 2014). doi.org/10.1002/arp.1483

Elliot, Daniel T. *Fort Hawkins: History and Archaeology.* Savannah, GA: LAMAR Institute, 2007.

Elliott, Daniel T., and Jack T. Wynn. "The Vining Revival: A Late Simple Stamped Phase in the Central Georgia Piedmont." *Early Georgia* 19 (1991): 1–18.

Fairbanks, Charles H. *Archaeology of the Funeral Mound, Ocmulgee National Monument, Georgia.* Tuscaloosa: University of Alabama Press, (1956) 2003.

———. "The Macon Earth Lodge." *American Antiquity* 12 (1946): 94–108.

Hally, David J. "Platform Mound Construction and the Instability of Mississippian Chiefdoms." In *Political Structure and Change in the Prehistoric Southeastern United States*. Edited by John F. Scarry. Gainesville: University Press of Florida, 1996.

Hally, David J., and Mark Williams. "Macon Plateau Site Community Pattern." In *Ocmulgee Archaeology 1936–1986*. Edited by David J. Hally. Athens: University of Georgia Press, 1994.

Jones, C. C. *Antiquities of the Southern Indians, Particularly of the Georgia Tribes*. Tuscaloosa: University of Alabama Press, (1873) 1999.

Kelly, Arthur R. *A Preliminary Report on Archaeological Explorations at Macon, Ga*. Bulletin 119, Bureau of American Ethnology, Anthropological Papers, No. 1. Washington DC: Smithsonian Institute, 1938.

King, Adam. *Etowah: The Political History of a Chiefdom Capital*. Tuscaloosa: University of Alabama Press, 2003.

Pluckhahn, Thomas J. "Rethinking Early Mississippian Chronology and Cultural Contact in Central Georgia: The View from Tarver (9JO6)." *Early Georgia* 25 (1997): 21–54.

Williams, Mark. "The Origins of the Macon Plateau Site." In *Ocmulgee Archaeology 1936–1986*. Edited by David J. Hally. Athens: University of Georgia Press, 1994.

———. *The View from Above: Archaeological Excavations at Brown's Mount*. Savannah, GA: LAMAR Institute, 1993.

Williams, Mark and Victor Thompson. "A Guide to Georgia Indian Pottery Types." *Early Georgia* 27 (1999):1–167.

Wilson, Gregory D. *The Archaeology of Everyday Life at Early Moundville*. Tuscaloosa: University of Alabama Press, 2008.